# CONTENTS

## SECTION 1

## SECTION 2

# Strings in Step

## piano
### accompaniments

### BOOK
### ONE

## Jan Dobbins

Music Department
OXFORD UNIVERSITY PRESS
Oxford and New York

# TEACHERS' NOTES

## Piano accompaniments  P

All tunes and exercises which have piano accompaniments are marked with the letter 'p' in the Pupil Books. The page number for the Pupil Book is given at the top of each piece in the Piano Book. Accompaniments are provided for all tunes and exercises in Book 1 with the following exceptions:

a) Exercises which cannot be played in ensemble with all instruments, i.e. p. 22; p. 24, exx. 1–4; p. 31; p. 49, exx. 1–3.

b) The rounds, which are best unaccompanied.

### The Open Strings Pizzicato (Pupil Book pages 10 and 11):

The accompaniments are lyrical and exciting enough for the pupils to feel that they are playing real pieces right from the start.

Later these pieces can be played with the bow.

### Pizzicato Tunes on the D String (Pupil Book page 13):

Accompaniments are given for all the tunes in E, A, D, G, and C majors so that pupils can practise using the finger pattern on each string as they become familiar with the tunes.

A tune using the second finger is included for cellists only.

The tunes can be played using the bow as pupils become more proficient. Some of the tunes appear further on in the book in notated form. The familiarity of these tunes encourages note reading.

The fourth finger is introduced on page 13. Violin and viola pupils can be encouraged to play the 'Fourth Finger March' regularly as preparation for the introduction of the fourth finger in Section 3.

### Bowing Patterns (Pupil Book page 19):

These can be introduced at the teacher's discretion. They are grouped together for convenience, but it is not necessary to cover them all at once.

When learning each of the major scales it is useful to play them using the bowing pattern rhythms. Examples of accompaniments for these are given in the keys of A, D, G, and C majors.

Jan Dobbins 1991

# SECTION 1

## Open Strings Pizzicato

**D String**

Pupil's Book p. 10

**A String**

**D & A Strings**

*Pizzicato in Waltz Time*

Pupil's Book p. 10

\* The violin part is given unless stated otherwise.

**E String**
**(violin only)**

Pupil's Book p. 11

**G and C Strings**

**All Four Strings**

## String Waltz

## Hopscotch

**D String**

**A String**

**E String**

## Hill Climbing

**D String**

**E String**

**G String**

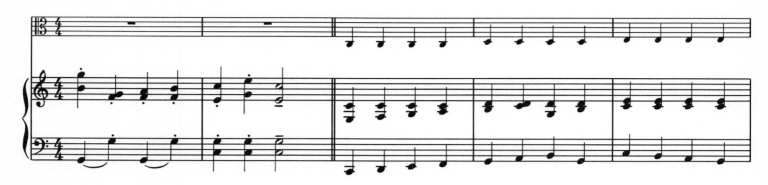

## Cello's Choice

**D String**

**A String**

**G String**

**C String**

## *Moonlight*

**D String**

**A String**

**E String**

**G String**

**C String**

## *Rainbows*

**D String**

**A String**

**E String**

**G String**

## Jumping Jack

**D String**

**A String**

**E String**

## Fourth Finger March

(violin and viola only)

**D String**

**A String**

**E String**

**G String**

# Scales Using the Bowing Patterns on Page 19

Al - to-ge-ther down up

**Pupil's Book p. 19**

**D Major**

I like je-lly ba-bies

\* These accompaniments are only to be used after the students have learnt the scales (pp. 35, 45, 49 and 59 in Pupil's Book One).

Al-to-ge-ther down up

**A Major**

I like je-lly ba-bies

**G Major**

Al-to-ge-ther down up

I like je-lly ba-bies

Al-to-ge-ther down up

**C Major**

I   like   je-lly ba-bies

# The Open Strings

**D String**

**A String**

**E String**
**(violas and cellos play C)**

**G String**

\* In the Pupil's books key signatures have not yet been introduced. Accidentals, when they occur, are placed before the notes. Here the key signatures have been added to the string part.

# The Minim

**D String**

**1.**

**A String**

**2.**

**E String (cellos and violas play C)**

**3.**

**G String**

**4.**

## *Minims on Two Strings*

## Bowing Exercises on Open Strings

## The Semibreve Rest

**Pupil's Book p. 25**

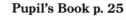

## The Minim Rest

## The Crotchet Rest

## The Rest Tests

1.

2.

# SECTION 2

## The First Finger on the D String

**Pupil's Book p. 28**

*First Finger Fiesta*

# The First Finger on the A String

**4.**

*Elegant Aunt Bertha*

Pupil's Book p. 29

Slowly

# The Second Finger on the D String

(cello only)

Pupil's Book p. 30

**1.**

**2.**

**(cello only)**

**3.**

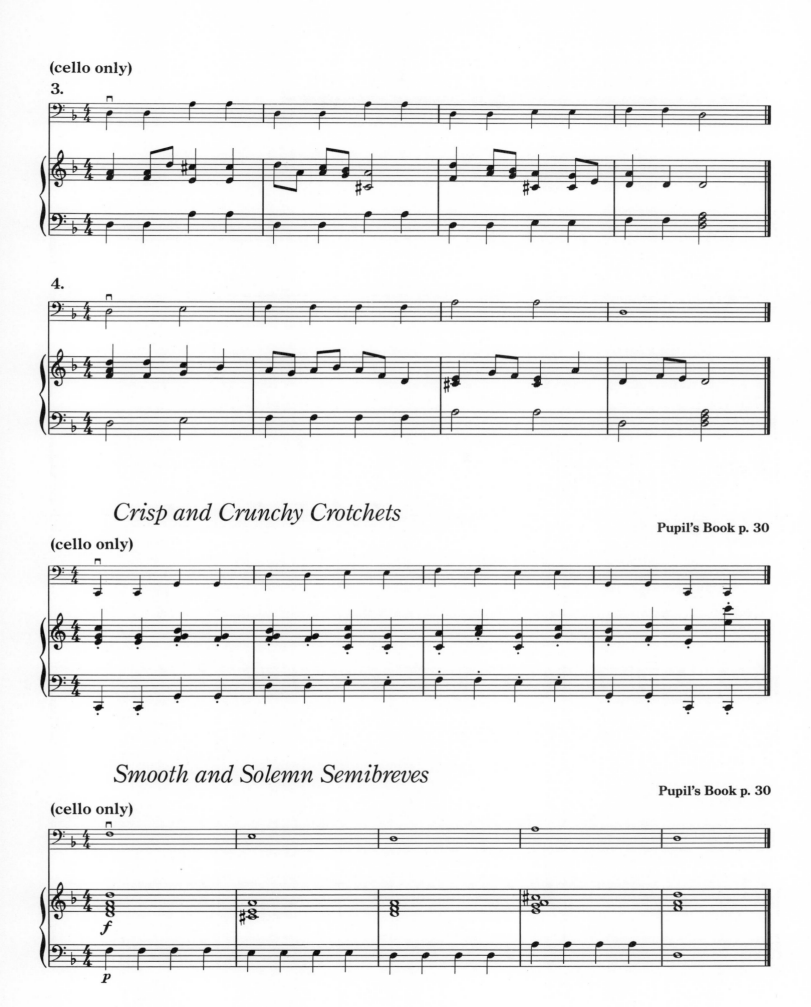

**4.**

## *Crisp and Crunchy Crotchets*

**Pupil's Book p. 30**

**(cello only)**

## *Smooth and Solemn Semibreves*

**Pupil's Book p. 30**

**(cello only)**

# The Second Finger on the A String

Pupil's Book p. 31

(cello only)

## *Mighty Minims on the Move*

**Pupil's Book p. 31**

(cello only)

# The Second Finger on the D String

**Pupil's Book p. 32**

(third finger for cellos)

## Going Shopping

Pupil's Book p. 32

## Sea Melody

Pupil's Book p. 32

# The Second Finger on the A String

(third finger for cellos)

Pupil's Book p. 33

## Hill and Valley March

**Pupil's Book p. 33**

## Snakes and Frogs

**Pupil's Book p. 33**

## I Hear Thunder

**Pupil's Book p. 33**

# The Third Finger on the D String

(fourth finger for cellos)

Pupil's Book p. 34

1.

2.

## Level Crossing

Pupil's Book p. 34

Smoothly

## Hill Climbing

Pupil's Book p. 34

*Rainbows*

Pupil's Book p. 34

# The Third Finger on the A String

(fourth finger for cellos)

Pupil's Book p. 35

## Third Finger First

Pupil's Book p. 35

## Swinging

Pupil's Book p. 35

Slowly

legato

## Jumping Jack

Pupil's Book p. 35

## Quavers

## Creeping Jenny

Pupil's Book p. 37

## Marigolds and Daisies

Pupil's Book p. 37

## I Like Caterpillars

Pupil's Book p. 37

marcato

## The Dotted Minim

**Pupil's Book p. 37**

## The Slur

**Pupil's Book p. 39**

1.

2.

## SECTION 3

*Twinkle, Twinkle Little Star*

Pupil's Book p. 41

## Frère Jacques

## Morris Tune

## London Bridge

Pupil's Book p. 42

## French Folk-song

Pupil's Book p. 42

## Exercises on the G String

Pupil's Book p. 45

**1.**

**2.**

*Moonlight*

**Pupil's Book p. 45**

*A Shady Lane*

**Pupil's Book p. 45**

## Buzzing Bees

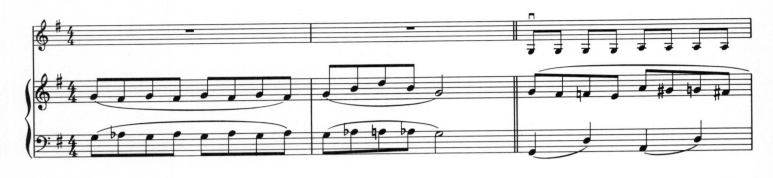

## Third Finger First

**(fourth finger first — cello)**

## Waltz in G

**Andante**

## Clog Dance

Pupil's Book p. 46

**Allegro**

## Exercises on the E (c) String

### *I Hear Thunder*

**Pupil's Book p. 49**

(violin)

### *I Hear Thunder*

**Pupil's Book p. 49**

(viola and cello)

### *Merry Dance*

**Pupil's Book p. 49**

## Satellite Serenade

Pupil's Book p. 49

## The Fourth Finger on the E String

### *The Fourth Finger Exercises*

**E String**
**(violin only)**

Pupil's Book p. 52

**A String**
**(violin and viola only)**

**D String**
**(viola only)**

## *Little Bird*

## Little Bird

**(cello only)**

Pupil's Book p. 53

## Moon Waltz

Pupil's Book p. 54